Sri Satya Sai Baba

Love and Truth, Inc.
2022.0922

Srinivas Shastri

*To my favorite uncle, **URK Murthi** గారు,*
who just turned 90,
*and **Ravishankar** & **Narayana**,*
two inspiring devotees of Swami

Ravishankar

"Uncle Moon is
everybody's uncle"
~The Gospel of Sri
Ramakrishna

Narayana

Swami outside our Pūja Room

अनन्याश्चिन्तयन्तो मां ये जनाः पर्युपासते |
तेषां नित्याभियुक्तानां योगक्षेमं वहाम्यहम् || 22||

ananyāśh chintayanto māṁ ye janāḥ paryupāsate
teṣhāṁ nityābhiyuktānāṁ yoga-kshemaṁ vahāmyaham

Men who worship me, thinking solely of me,
always disciplined, win the reward I secure
~Bhagavad Gita 9:22

In Gratitude

With heartfelt thanks to:

- Mal, for communicating the *adēsh* [command] from Shirdi Sai Baba, which initiated a series of blooks [a blook is a printed book that contains or is based on content from a blog]
- Ravishankar and Narayana, who showed what a true follower of Swami's teachings could be like
- The **Holy Bhagavad Gita** site [https://www.holy-bhagavad-gita.org/] for the snippets that i have used, with translations by Barbara Stoler Miller
- My chromeOS devices, Asus Chromebox 4 and HP Chromebook, which made writing this blook in Google Docs such a breeze

Notes

- **Swami** refers to Satya Sai Baba
- **Shirdi Baba** refers to **Sai Baba of Shirdi**
- The **Master** refers to Sri Ramakrishna
  - The **Gospel** refers to **The Gospel of Sri Ramakrishna**
- **Ramanachala** refers to Sri Ramana Maharshi
- **Boldfacing** in quotes used is by the author, unless otherwise specified
- This document uses US spellings and follows the Times of India Edit Page style of using the lower-case **i**, except at the start of sentences. The Big I refers to the Self, in which all things appear and disappear
- All photos/images are shot/made by the author, unless otherwise indicated; a link either to the pic or web page will be provided, where possible
- The plural of *Indian words* will be the same word; suffixing them with an **s** seems to be a travesty
- Names from Indian history might not be italicized
- **TeJo** refers to tears of joy, which flow from the **outer** corners of the eyes
- AUCoE refers to Andhra University College of Engineering, Vizag
- WIMWI refers to IIM, Ahmedabad
- PM refers to our gated community in Whitefield
- Feel that the period is superfluous at the end of paragraphs

Table of Contents

https://youtu.be/GQLI2l_n3gU

Screenshot from *Tapōvanam* in Telugu~Chapter 18

Introduction

Valentine's Day has a different ring for me

It was on that day in 1993 that i experienced the powerful look of Swami. I had gone to Brindavan, Whitefield along with my spouse and there was a big crowd, as usual. I got some space in the open area, on the right side of Sai Ramesh hall, and, due to some reason, Swami came to that side. He wasn't more than 20 feet away when He looked right **into** me. Still to recover from that yogic glance, even though it happened almost thirty years ago

As a result of that look, i am not really that interested in photos of Swami where He's **not** looking at the camera. But the ones that do **very easily** fill me with bliss

The life of Swami has been well documented and will **not** be the subject of this blook. Enough material exists on the Net such as:

https://en.wikipedia.org/wiki/Sathya_Sai_Baba

The reader can also refer to some of the following books, which have been my inspiration for long

https://flic.kr/p/axtaNR

https://flic.kr/p/2kwXmhi

తపోవనం ~ *Tapōvanam* in Telugu

This blook will be the **intersection** of material on Swami and how He affected me through dreams, experiences, and ideas

Sai Baba Mandir in PM

According to the *Śakti* cult the *siddha* is called a *koul*, and according to the *Vedānta*, a *paramahamsa*. The Bauls call him a sai. They say, 'No one is greater than a sai.' The sai is a man of supreme perfection. He doesn't see any differentiation in the world. He wears a necklace, one half made of cow bones and the other of the sacred *tulsi*-plant [Holy Basil]. He calls the Ultimate Truth *Ālekh*, the 'Incomprehensible One'. The Vedas call It 'Brahman'. About the *jīva* the Bauls say, 'They come from *Ālekh* and they go unto *Ālekh*.' That is to say, the individual soul has come from the Unmanifest and goes back to the Unmanifest

~The **Gospel**, Chapter **27. At Dakshineswar**

Listening to the Silence

Way back in 1991~1992, while working at TCS, stayed with a couple in Besant Nagar, Chennai as a Paying Guest (PG)

Both their sons had moved on, so they let out the two rooms in the upper floor of their villa to PGs. My fellow PG was out traveling most of the time, so i had the upper floor to myself. Uncle had a sweet Guruvayoorappan photo in the common area there, where he would come up and light the lamp late in the night

Used to hang around there and think of the Old Mother and Her many weird numbers, like the Goliath Beetle, and pass the time

Sell your cleverness and buy bewilderment~Rumi

During one such episode, was **seized** with the thought that one should understand what It was all about. Was about to do the nightly brush at that point and the toothpaste came out in a funny way: one half came out, a plop, followed by the other half. Couldn't make much head or tail out of it

Everything happens in time, that funny thing that prevents everything from happening at the same time :-)

Early April 2006, was sort of recollecting this episode. The very next day, was going through an experience of a Ramanachala devotee, when i read the following:

> I picked up the book *Jnāna Vashistha* and began reading it from beginning to end with the hope of finding the solution to my dilemma. I continued reading without eating the whole day. In the evening the answer came: a stanza in *Jnāna Vashistha* said: "Between two thoughts there is an interval of no thought. That interval is the Self, the *Ātman*. It is pure Awareness only"

Eckhart Tolle notes: When Ramanachala was asked how to gauge one's own spiritual progress, He said by the degree of absence of thought

Papaji writes of Ramanachala:

When I was at
Ramanasramam in the
1940s I used to spend
hours looking at the
Maharshi's eyes. They
would be open and staring,
but not focused on
anything. Though his eyes
were open, they were not
seeing anything. **Those
eyes were completely
free of thoughts and
desires.** The mind is
revealed very clearly in the
eyes, but in those eyes
there was nothing at all to
see. In the hours that I
concentrated on his eyes, I
didn't once see even a
flicker of a thought or a
desire. I have not seen
such utterly desire-less
eyes like his on any other
face. I have met many
great saints during my life,
but no one has impressed
me as much as the
Maharshi did

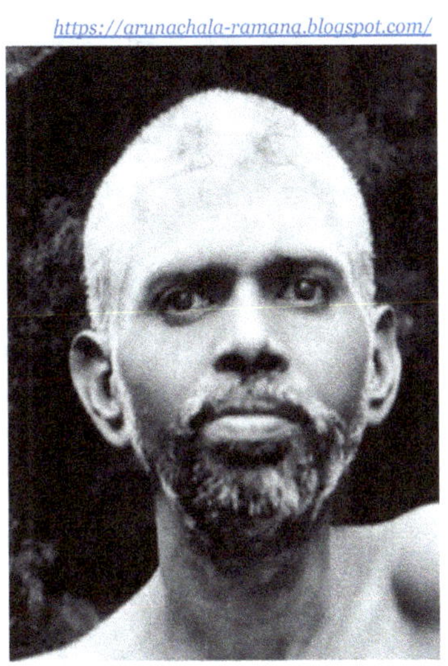

Those who cannot understand His silence, will not understand His words!
~Shivkumar Sharma

Gopa, my childhood pal, observed: "Like in a spark plug, I guess we need that gap for the spark!"

No wonder i was so impressed with the titling of **FaSTeR** by James Gleick: [https://g.co/kgs/cjz4Ap]

Without the breathing space of the vowels, life is no fun

ESOP on the birthday of Swami

பொன் கிடைத்தாலும் புதன் கிடைக்காது
[You might get gold but not a Wednesday that easily]
~ Tamil saying

A year after the yogic glance, i received the warrants, vesting after five years, for the ESOP [Employee Stock Ownership Plan] from the Infosys top brass:

- Nandan Nilekani, one of the founders of Infosys
- AK Khurana [AKK], who was the head of Banking Business Unit [BBU]

It was a Wednesday and the birthday of Swami [23rd November] in 1994

Nandan and AKK led three of us [HPR, RSR, *et moi*] into the far conference room at Infosys "Pink" Building, Koramangala

I didn't know this ESOP thing from Adam then, but RSR held forth on what a **great** thing that Infosys was doing. After a while, Nandan gave him a look as if wondering when RSR would shut up. I got 800, the same number as RSR

No way i was going to take that number: Wouldn't 'ouch an 8 with a bargepole

Later, i asked Nandan, who was an epitome of **Management by Wandering Around** [https://g.co/kgs/s1RXcC], whether i could take **720**; CPKK, the chap who taught me numerology, used to say that **72** was the number of Kubera [the God of Wealth] and that it was always a good idea to open a bank account starting with 72... [and ending with as many zeroes as feasible]

Nandan said that i could take only a **multiple** of 100

And that's what i did. While giving in the acceptance document, MDPai, the Infosys CFO, said that i was crazy to let go of the 100. Asked him whether there was any issue if i took lesser. He said No. So i ended up with the reverse of James Bond

As it turned out, both HPR and self cashed while RSR, who was giving all that spiel, couldn't. Needless to say, he opted for the entire number he was offered

So, even though i might be fooling around with numerology for fun, you never know when it might come in **really** handy, in the absence of other data in taking a decision

Do i regret missing on the 💯? No!

Around 2020, when i shared this story with the BBU Pioneers, my pal CSP calculated how many shares the 💯, which i had sacrificed on the altar of numerology, would have become with all the bonus issues and one stock split in the interim years: **51,200** shares!

But i still felt that i made the right call, as **51,200** adds up to yet another 8!

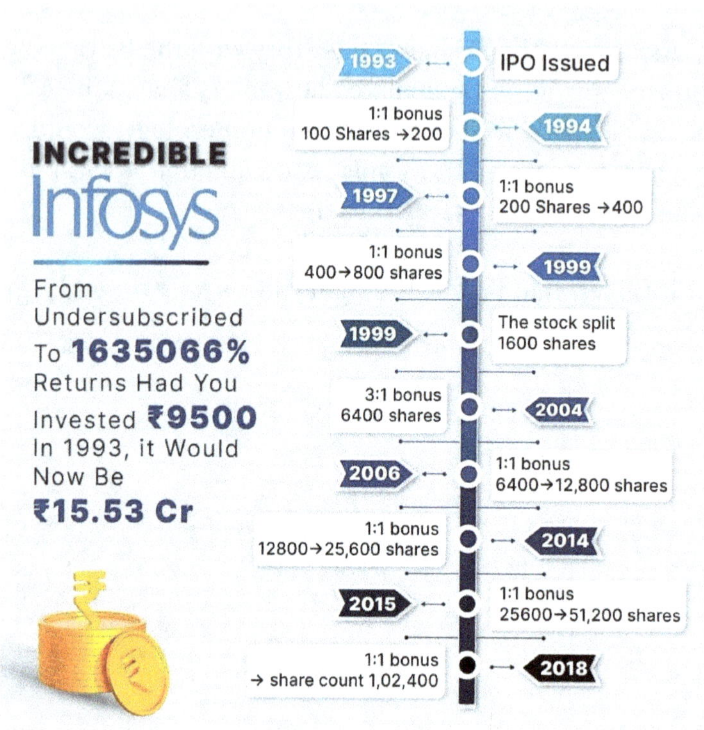

via WhatsApp

Sri Sai Seva Trust, Srirangapatna

We visited this place on Saturday 4th September 2004. Photos have been taken when we revisited the place on Monday 19th May 2008

The first Saturday in September 2004, went on a nice one-day trip to Sai Seva Trust, located a few kilometers on the main road from Srirangapatna to Mysore

Assembled early in the morning Chez Sampath uncle, which is becoming more & more a focus for Swami's activities. After 21 ॐ *Omkār*, an *ārati* was given for the Swaraj Mazda van and we all started off, with quite a few kids in tow. All told, there were about 20 members of families that usually participate in the daily Sai *bhajan* sessions at PM

Soon after we hit the Mysore road, the going was slow due to heavy traffic and a lot of work being done on the Bengaluru~Mysuru highway. What a contrast it was compared to other highways that one has gotten used to. To top it all, at a traffic snarl, our driver blocked the oncoming traffic with his unnecessary lane-jumping tactics and, sitting behind the driver, we were subjected to some choice abuses from all the drivers once the jam cleared

Heard a very nice incident from Savitri, who was seated at the front along with us: one of the Sai devotees had just dropped off her husband at the airport and came back home. When she went into the bedroom, she found Swami reclining on the bed. She had barely recovered from her shock, when Swami exhorted her to keep singing bhajans, before disappearing! Later on, she clarified that this happened in a dream

Stopped at a nice place for breakfast, where we had piping-hot *thaṭē idli, vaḍa,* and set *dōsa,* washed down by some strong coffee. There were so many people ordering so many things that it was a wonder that the restau got its billing right. Weirdly enough, turkeys were playing in the lot, right behind the restau. Still some days to go for Thanksgiving!

After breakfast, folks got some enthusiasm to sing *bhajan.* However, it soon moved on to *antākshari.* Having slept for just four hours earlier in the night, i was interested in getting some shut-eye, but that was more a pipedream, what with the seats being so cramped

Ramanagaram, Channapatna, Maddur, and Mandya were a memory as we reached the Sai Seva Trust. You could miss it if you aren't careful. However, it's much more visible coming from the Mysuru side towards Bengaluru. If you are crossing a bridge over the Kaveri river and, on the left, you see a huge photo of Swami overlooking a building complex, that's the place

Sri Sai Seva Trust, Srirangapatna

Folks soon got down to a *bhajan* session in the *mandir*, which had some really old photos of Swami, Shirdi Sai, and even those of the Holy Trio [Sri Ramakrishna, Holy Mother Sri Sarada Devi, and Swami Vivekananda]. I particularly liked a soulful painting of Naga Sai [Shirdi Sai under a five-hooded snake], which I focused on during the *bhajan*

The *bhajan* session was meandering for a while till *Allah Bhajo*, which perked me up. This was followed by a powerful rendition of *Bhashma Bhushitanga Sai Chandrashekhara*. *Subramaniam, Subramaniam* was soon after, indicating the end of the *bhajan* session. I'm

yet to hear *Subramaniam, Subramaniam* sung as
interestingly as Swami does

Vibhūti on Swami's Photo

Sampath uncle pointed to the photo of Swami on which *vibhūti* manifests itself. The face in the picture is kept clear, revealing a charming Swami in His youth, looking like an Eskimo! Even as i watched, *vibhūti* started forming in the area of His left temple! We got a couple of packets of the *vibhūti* home; it smells divine

Sri Alagappan, the caretaker of the Trust, started
distributing the *amrutam* [nectar]. This manifests itself
from two Sai "dollars", one of Shirdi Sai and the other of
Swami. I went outside to wash my hands

There was a huge photo of Swami, eyes shining in that limpid way, grinning away and, with His flying hair, making Him look like a happy lion. I am not at all surprised that some of His appearances were like Narasimha Swami

Smiling (Narasimha) Swami

By the time i went back in, giving the *amrutam* from the dollars was suspended and i had to be content with the regular *amrutam* given from a vessel. It had an amazing taste. Later on, Sampath uncle was mentioning that Sri Alagappan doesn't offer the *amrutam* to many people using the dollars. Guess one gets what one deserves. We got back some home

The story of Sri Alagappan is interesting: He was a
Naxalite, who had given up that activity after he visited
Swami in 1945. After three years at Puttaparthi, Swami
asked him to go back to the banks of the Kaveri. When Sri
Alagappan came to Srirangapatna, a high chair was waiting
for him, with the two dollars on it, oozing the *amrutam*

Heard that it all started with Sri Alagappan finding a small
enamel piece of Swami's picture in the 1970s in
Puttaparthi. Miraculously, *amrutam* started forming from
this pendant

We later walked down to the banks of the Kaveri. Wiped
my handkerchief on the *pāduka*, kept slightly above the
water line. In times of flood, they say that the waters wash
the *pāduka*. Later that evening, at the badminton court,
when i asked some of my friends to smell the 'kerchief, they
found the smell heavenly

Rajan was mentioning that some of the crocodiles had
wandered down from the Ranganathittu Bird Sanctuary
upstream and that the water wasn't safe. My kid started
seeing crocs instead of underwater rocks from then on!

On the way back, it was a state of torpor till JanaPadaLoka
[i refer to it as JPL!], which serves some awesome *jowar
rōṭi*. Upgraded my lunch from the two-*rōṭi* plate to the
unlimited-*rōṭi thāli*

It was the wedding anniversary of the lady who saw Swami in the bedroom [in the dream] and she ordered *gulāb jāmun* for all. Was touched by her generous spirit; guess that's what Swami means by the line "Expansion is My Life" in the song "Love is My Form"

Sat with the kids at the back of the van and played some word games. What's the English word whose plural doubles in length? Kids are pretty smart nowadays. With some clues, they could guess that it was Ox/Oxen and Ax/Axes

Then it was back to some snoozing. Fortunately, i got up in time to notice that the driver had taken the wrong turn at the junction of the Outer Ring Road and Bannerghatta Road; he was headed for the Bannerghatta zoo! We made it back home by 6:30 PM, giving folks enough time to freshen up for the daily *bhajan* session at 7 PM

Bad roads and a cramped van couldn't keep one from enjoying a spiritually-enriching trip

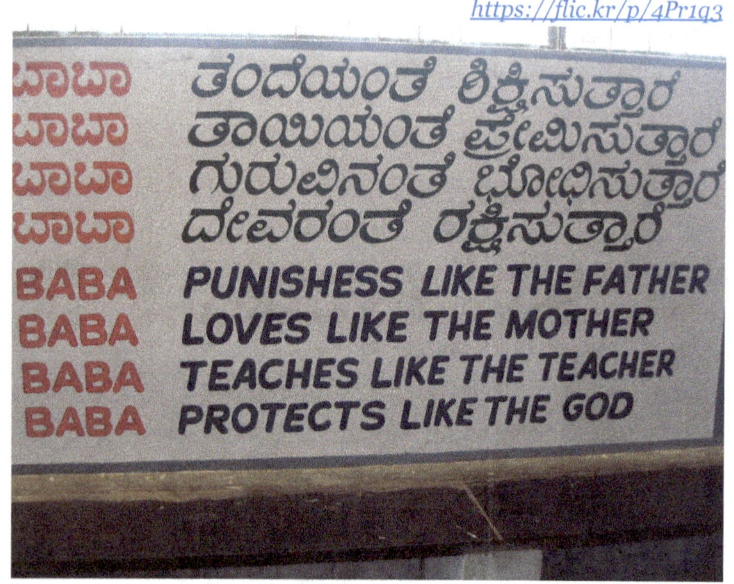

Swami in various *avatār*

Letter to The Week on their "80th birthday of Swami" issue

Thanks for your neutral reporting on the eve of the 80th birthday of Swami

In his book on **Ramakrishna and His Disciples**, Christopher Isherwood talks of the importance of experience in spiritual life as that can **never** be taken away from one. This later on triggered:

> *The Infinite One*
> *Cannot be Understood*
> *Only Experienced*

Swami is like That. Some of my experiences:

- Swami looking right into my eyes, interestingly enough, on Valentine's Day in 1993
- Getting the Infosys ESOP on His birthday in 1994, which enabled me to buy a villa in the most well-known gated complex in Bengaluru
- Seeing a huge dark cloud at Puttaparthi (referred to as "Put-apart-the-I" by Swami) and noticing that it was in the shape of Swami looking down at His abode
- One of the more interesting dreams is the Flying Dream, where one feels that one is flying, including

maneuvering in the sky. I have had this dream a
few times in my Life and it's always a great feeling.
In one instance, Swami was massaging the calf of
my leg and, soon after, i had a flying dream that
filled me with exhilaration
- The Third Eye of Swami

Even though many indicators have been given about
Swami being the messiah (Kalki, Hazrat Mehdi), nothing is
more striking to me than the experience narrated on page
42 of Evelyne Blau's stunning and lovingly-produced
Krishnamurti: 100 Years [https://g.co/kgs/qmppJm].
The incident is as follows:

On December 28, 1925, a unique occurrence took place
at which I was present. At a meeting of the Star
Congress under the banyan tree in Adyar at 8 o'clock in
the morning, with the amplifiers turned off, a dramatic
event took place while Krishnaji was speaking. It came
at the end of his talk. He has been speaking about the
world teacher; suddenly his voice changed to an
exquisitely sweet yet powerful tone and, through great
waves of compassionate power, he continued: "He
comes only to those who want, who desire, who
long"—and then it became a different voice—calm,
serene and with a ringing quality. He said: "I come for
those who want sympathy, who want happiness, who
are longing to be released, who are longing to find
happiness in all things. I come to reform and not to
tear down. I come not to destroy but to build"

Love and Truth, Inc.

... In the ninety-second year of my life my memory is probably defective, but I do recall this unforgettable experience with crystal clarity

—Russell Balfour Clarke

This happened on Monday 28th December 1925, just a few months before the birth of Swami on Tuesday 23rd November 1926

I have no doubt whatsoever that the voice "Calm, serene and with a ringing quality" belongs to Swami. I felt such joy the first time i heard Swami speak!

The words "I come to reform and not to tear down. I come not to destroy but to build" reflect much of what Swami has done

Even after 12 years, i can still feel the power behind that look in 1993

"Third Eye" of Swami

The sun was streaming in through the curtains on our backyard French windows and, by a quirk, formed a nice round *bindi* on the forehead of Swami on the cover of **Divine Journey**. Had to scramble to take the photo; the *bindi* disappeared within two minutes

Advent of Swami

Like in the case of Jesus of Nazareth, have heard of two other instances of Immaculate Conception

In the case of the Master, one reads:

> Remarkably, Sri Ramakrishna manifested himself in the world in exactly the same way as Lingodbhava Siva. A flood of divine light emerged out of Sivalinga at Kamarpukur and entered the body of Chandramani Devi, who thereafter fell unconscious when she was on the point of telling the blacksmith woman Dhani about it. Dhani helped Chandramani recover and was surprised to hear about her wonderful experience. Chandramani had the feeling that the light of Siva was in her womb and that she was pregnant

In the case of Swami, one reads:

Years later as Swami sat one day surrounded by His
devotees, there was an abrupt interruption. A pundit,
well-versed in the holy *purāṇa* felt a sudden urge to ask
a question: "Swami! Was your incarnation a *pravēśam*
[advent] or a *prasavam* [normal conception]?" I could
not quite understand the relevance of the interruption
that jolted everybody away from the jocular mood of
the talk, but Swami knew the reason. Turning to
Easwaramma [His Mother] seated in front, He said,
"Tell Rama Sarma what happened that day near the
well after your mother-in-law had warned you."
Mother said, "She had dreamt of Satyanarayana Deva
and He cautioned me that I should not be frightened if
something happens to me through the will of God.
That morning when I was at the well drawing water, a
big ball of blue light came rolling toward me and I
fainted and fell. I felt, it glided into me." Swami turned
to Rama Sarma with a smile: "There you have the
answer. I was not begotten. It was *pravēśam*, not
prasavam"

Two Little Masters

Sachin (fourth from left) with Swami

For folks who were surprised to see Sachin Tendulkar at the 80th birthday celebrations of Swami in 2005, Sunil Gavaskar writes in the 75th Birthday issue (November 2000) of **Sanathana Sarathi**: (page 345)

A few years later, I was privileged to arrange the players for the Unity Cup Cricket Match. Swami has always said, "Life is a game. Play it." Bhagavan wanted to show that there could be unity among different countries, cultures, and communities through sports. So, the Unity Cup was played with players from all over the world, including Pakistan

Several senior retired players were honored and had the good fortune to be blessed by Bhagavan

Who can forget Bhagavan patting Sachin Tendulkar on the back and telling him, "I am with you!"

What a season Sachin had after that as he virtually single-handedly demolished World Champions Australia with his batting that seemed to be of a totally different dimension after that pat from Bhagavan!

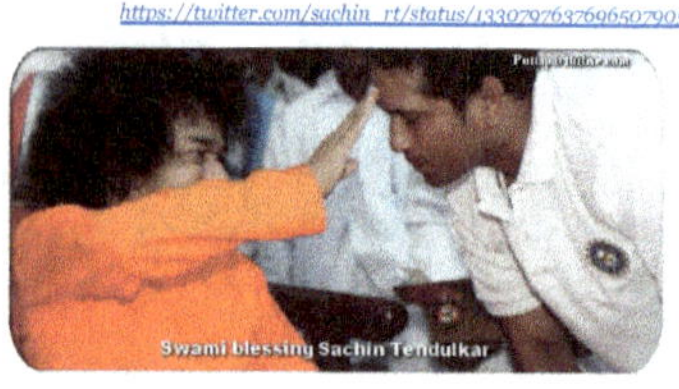

I remember the final being played on the 25th birthday (24th April 1998) of Tendulkar. In the morning, i was attending an HP seminar on data warehousing. The speaker was an Aussie and he was gloating on the pasting that the OZs were gonna give us. Too bad none of us retorted; anyway, Sachin did that for us later on in the day!

Bhajan Cornucopia

Had some serious luck on *Sri Rāma Navami* [27th March] in 2007

Went to Brindavan, the *āshram* of Swami in Whitefield, Bengaluru, along with my FiL [father-in-law] for the *Sri Rāma Navami bhajan* session, but we were a bit late

However, we checked out their book shop [open till noon] and ended up buying:

- A nice *Bāl Vikas* diary for 2007
- **108 Magical Moments**
- **ARMY** (9th~19th August 2006)
- **Satyam Sivam Sundaram** Volumes I to V
- *Tapōvanam*

When we came out, some of the shops were playing some songs from the Sundaram Bhajan Group; so we went over. Have the Volume I by the same group and love those *bhajan*. My favorite is the 15th one, with that lovely two-second riff at the end of it:

Jaya Ho Sai Ram Jaya Ho Sai Ram
Karuna Sindhu Ram Sai Parthi Pureeshwara Ram
Treta Yugame Ram Sai Dwapara Yugame Shyam
Ram Thu Hi Rahman Sai Sab Ka Hai Bhagavan
Kali Yuga Ke Avatar Sai Parthi Pureeshwara Ram

In the absence of other info, we bought Volumes 5 and 14 for ₹100 each, since i feel that 5 is the number of the Self. Suggested Volume 1 for FiL, but the vendor was pooh-poohing it, recommending Volume 2 instead. It turned out that he didn't have Volume 1. Heh

https://flic.kr/p/85hbjz

Sundaram Sai Bhajan

The "MP³" on the inlay card isn't a mistake!

When i came out, heard the neighboring vendor playing Volume 1, so i was wondering what the deal was. He said that he had an MP3 of **10** Sundaram Bhajan albums (1~8, 13~14), comprising 163 songs, all for just ₹170. That's like ~INR 1 for each bhajan, much cooler than the Apple iTunes rate

Why do i attend *bhajan* sessions?

After his meeting with Sri Ramakrishna, M., the author of the **Gospel**, made a beeline to Dakshineswar for his next meeting. The Master joked:

> A man once fed a peacock with a pill of opium at four o'clock in the afternoon. The next day, exactly at that time, the peacock came back. It had felt the intoxication of the drug and returned just in time to have another dose

The reason i attend *bhajan* sessions is somewhat similar. Get into a high, without having to snort anything! Swami says:

> The spiritual vibrations produced by Bhajans confer great joy both on those who sing them and on those who listen to them. Bhajans remove all negative thoughts, soothe the nerves, purify the mind and fill the body and the heart with sweet love for the divine. As one sings Bhajans, the mind is saturated with God Consciousness and a great ecstasy wells up from within. No mental or intellectual effort is called for, as there is no need to understand anything while uttering the holy names of God and singing His glory. The singing and the atmosphere created by Bhajans takes one beyond the realms of the body, mind and intellect and helps to establish communion with the Higher Self (consciousness) within

In 2007, we celebrated the birthday of Swami. The photo was very nicely decorated

Lots of folks were there, with a few new faces. Never know what to expect from them

bhajan: bhāv [feeling]
with jan [people]

The person to my "North East", Sri Srikantan of Chennai, sang a tremendous Siva bhajan (*Bhasma Bhooshitanga Sai Chandrasekara*), which made me cry with joy at the start itself. He sang a small intro song before the bhajan (generally not done), which had some of the regular singers looking askance, but as they say, "my karma ran over your dogma"! Anything that makes you cry with joy

In that wonderful chapter on the Swami in **God Lived with Them**, we read: (page 136)

When I first started visiting the Master, I often felt inclined to cry. One night I was crying uncontrollably by the riverside near the *bakul* [Spanish cherry] tree. The Master was in his room, and he inquired where I had gone. When I returned he asked me to sit down and said: "The Lord is greatly pleased if one cries to him. **Tears of love wash away the mental impurities accumulated through the ages**. It is very good to cry to God"

Another day when I was meditating in the Panchavati grove, my concentration became very deep. The Master came towards me from the pine grove, and as soon as he looked at me, I burst into tears. The Master stood still. I felt something creeping up inside my chest, and I was overcome by a fit of shaking. The Master said that my crying was not insignificant. It was a type of ecstasy

https://flic.kr/p/3ahmDb

The Master makes a wonderful allusion in the Gospel:
(Chapter **3. Visit to Vidyasagar**)

64WV+8R2, Omkareshwar, MP

Vishwaroopa Darshan at
**Annapurna Mata
Mandir**

Chaitanyadeva set out on a pilgrimage to southern India. One day he saw a man reading the Gita. Another man, seated at a distance, was listening and weeping. His eyes were swimming in tears. Chaitanyadeva asked him, 'Do you understand all this?' The man said, 'No, revered sir, I don't understand a word of the text.' 'Then why are you crying?' asked Chaitanya. The devotee said: 'I see Arjuna's chariot before me. I see Lord Krishna and Arjuna seated in front of it, talking. I see this and I weep'

Unmana

The Sai Bhajan Cornucopia still sounds very fresh

Around Jan 2015, started culling my absolute favorites, which make me cry, and made a playlist:

1. Ganesha: *Sundara Sundara Vināyaka*
2. Guru: *Sai Baba Gīta Sudha*
3. Shiva: *Chandrashekharāya Namah Om*
4. Old Mother: *Hey Rambha Janani*
5. Rama: *Raghupatē Rāghava*
6. Krishna: *Mana Mōhana Shyāma Murāri*
7. The Underlying Consciousness: *Brahmamokkaṭē*

The name for the playlist was sort of self-evident: *unmana*

The Master uses this word to describe a particular type of *samādhi*, when the dispersed mind suddenly comes together

In the **Gospel**, we find the Master telling M.: (Chapter **17. M. at Dakshineswar~I**)

> "There is another kind of *samādhi*, called *unmana samādhi*. One attains it by suddenly gathering the dispersed mind. You understand what that is, don't you?"

In **The Fabric of Life**, on the Songs of the Mystic Kabir, Osho comments:

> Just as *brahman*, the Infinite, is hidden in each and everything, similarly the divine presence is hidden in everybody; it is hidden in you too. The name Kabir has given to that divine presence is very significant. It is the same one as the Zen mystics have given it in Japan. Zen mystics call it a state of no-mind. Kabir calls the same state *unmani* — a state of consciousness where the mind is no more

"Swamadhi" of Ramanachala

Balan, my friend in spirit, is a devotee of Ramanachala. Both of us planned to hit the lovely road to Tiruvannamalai on 14th April in 2007. The date is auspicious for Tamilians; it's their New Year Day

It's also the day Ramanachala attained *mahāsamādhi* in the year 1950

There's a stunning incident associated with it. A Swami devotee named Varadu reports what happened: (**Love is My Form**, page 497, bottom)

...the night when Ramana Maharshi passed away in Tiruvannamalai, I was with Swamiji. Krishna [another young devotee] and myself were both there. That evening, around 9:00, we continued whatever it was that we were doing (I think we were doing a *pūja*) when suddenly Swamiji looked up at us. There was a peculiar way of looking he has which means that he wants to go to his room. The moment Krishna and I went through

the door into the room and closed it, Swami fell down.
I was ready for it. Krishna and I both held hands, and
Swami was lying across them. Then [He]...rose up into
the air, from our arms. He was as stiff as a board. He
started murmuring—something about 'Maharshi has
reached my lotus feet'. And then the sole of
[His]...right foot split open, and nearly two kilograms
of beautiful, well-scented *vibhūti* poured out from the
sole of his foot. I collected the *vibhūti* while [He]...was
still levitating in the air

Then [He]...came down and returned to [His]...senses
and asked what [He]...had said. I said, "Swamiji, this is
what you said: 'Ramana Maharshi has passed away.'
And this is what came out of your feet." He said: 'Put it
into packets and give it as *prasādam*'

A day or two after this incident, we learned from the
newspapers that Maharshi had died. It had been at the
time that Swami said that Maharshi had reached
[His]...feet

Baba's *kafni*

There's an interesting story on Baba's *kafni* [cowl] in Chapter 5 of the **Shri Sai Satcharita**:

> There was a wrestler in Shirdi, by name Mohdin Tamboli. Baba and he did not agree on some items, and both had a fight. In this Baba was defeated. Thenceforth, Baba changed His dress and mode of living. He donned *kafni*, wore a *langōt* [waist band], and covered His head with a piece of cloth. He took a piece of sack-cloth for His seat, sack-cloth for His bed, and was content with wearing torn and worn-out rags. He always said that "Poverty is better than Kingship, far better than Lordship. The Lord is always brother [befriender] of the poor"

I find it unusual that Baba lost. The same story, with the roles [of winner and loser] reversed, was presented by Swami on Sunday 4th March 1962, during a speech on the occasion of the MahaShivaRatri festival: (**The Life and Teachings of Sai Baba of Shirdi**, page 67)

I am reminded now of past events, events in my previous body. Even then, I had Sathya or Truth as my Support. A wrestler challenged Me for a fight and he was defeated before a large gathering of villagers. Pained by the insult, he invited Baba for a second tussle the next day, so that he might win back his lost reputation. The man swore that if defeated again, he would wear a long rough *kafni* and move about with his head covered in cloth. He dared Baba too to swear like-wise. Baba was in no mood to enter the arena again and he was quite prepared to concede the fellow the victory he craved. So he accepted defeat and himself donned the *kafni* and the kerchief. The wrestler felt great remorse and his insolence melted away. He appealed to Baba to resume his usual style of dress and released him from the obligation. But Baba stuck to his word. He was Sathya Itself. Then, as He is now, He wore the new attire

What i like most about Baba's *kafni* is this observation:

Shirdi Baba's *kafni*, which came to his knees due to his height, covers Swami **fully**

Śrēyas versus prēyas

Remember always that it is easy to do what is pleasant; but it is difficult to be engaged in what is beneficial. Not all that is pleasant is profitable. Success comes to those who give up the path strewn with roses, and brave the hammer-blows and sword-thrusts of the path fraught with danger
*~**Sathya Sai Speaks**, Vol. 3, Ch. 18*
(Krishna Janmaashtami, 12th August 1963)

One thing that i do of late is the classification of activities into the *śrēyas* and the *prēyas*, i.e., the good and the pleasant

Lord Yama raises the same with Nachiketa in the **Katha Upanishad**: (start of chapter 2, Part One)

Yama said: The good is one thing; the pleasant, another. Both of these, serving different needs, bind a man. It goes well with him who, of the two, takes the good; but he who chooses the pleasant misses the end

Both the good and the pleasant present themselves to a man. The calm soul examines them well and discriminates. Yea, he prefers the good to the pleasant; but the fool chooses the pleasant out of greed and avarice

There's a reference to it in Chapters 16&17 of the **Shri Sai Satcharita** as well:

> Qualifications for *Brahma-Jnāna* or Self-Realization
> ...
> (6) Preferring *śrēyas* (the Good) to *prēyas* (the Pleasant). There are two sorts of things viz., the Good and the Pleasant; the former deals with spiritual affairs, and the latter with mundane matters. Both these approach man for acceptance. He has to think and choose one of them. The wise man prefers the Good to the Pleasant; but the unwise, through greed and attachment, chooses the Pleasant

A simple example: you are peeling a pomegranate. Do you eat the peeled stuff in between or at the end? Find that i can't really pop in the stuff in between but more at the end, as a sort of reward for the good work done

Boil the milk or oil the blog? Earlier i would have plonked down in front of the computer. But now it's the milk first; in fact, all that time in the kitchen is a good fermenting ground for "mule"ing over future writing

The person who chooses the *śrēyas* finds that there's always something good to do. And if you can add a dash of Osho while doing that good thing, what more can one want?

Be Creative, Do Small Acts With Love

...

A man of understanding is continuously creative. Not that he is trying to be creative. The way he sits is a creative act. Watch him sitting. You will find in his movement a certain quality of dance, a certain dignity. Life consists of small things; just your ego goes on saying these are small things. You would like to do some great thing — great poetry. You would like to become Shakespeare, Kalidas, or Milton. It is your ego that is creating the trouble

Drop the ego and everything is creative. Then everything is tremendously great. If you don't love, then your ego goes on saying, "This is not worthy of you." Cleaning is great. Don't go on an ego trip. Whenever the ego comes and persuades you towards some great things, immediately become aware and drop the ego, and then by and by you will find trivia sacred. Nothing is profane; everything is sacred and holy

Milk Sachets Make the Olympic Cachet, on the Opening ceremony day of the 29th Olympics games in Beijing: **8/8/8** [Friday 8th August 2008]

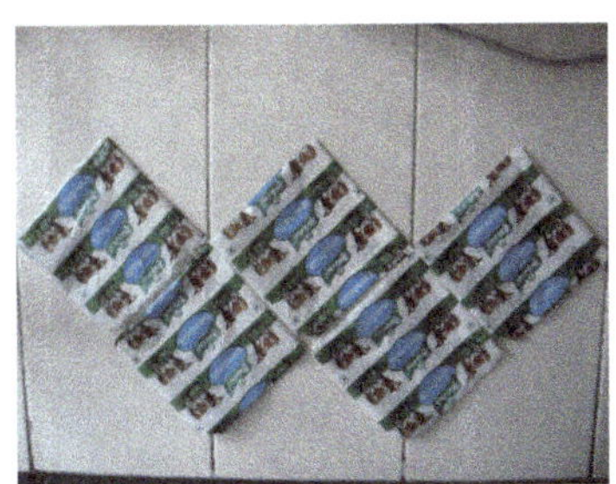

This a++itude [choosing the good over the pleasant] has significant benefits

Am always impressed with myself when i finish things before rather than later. Finish the work and rest peacefully

As one of the direct disciples of the Master said:

What you want to do tomorrow, do it today
What you want to do today, do it now!

And no one has to applaud either, ridding oneself of the tyranny of expectations

As my dear friend PSM observed so sagely:

When you satisfy the job,
you might get job satisfaction

And pat myself on the back for a job well done

The Ghost Who Walks

Unadhikakritamkritam
The best ghost short that i have read

It's that time of the year again [Halloween 2008] and most of our gated community is gearing up for the 🎃 do in the evening

Folks started getting ready a few days earlier, as i saw on one of my cycling rounds

A House for Halloween

One night last month, we were all discussing whether ghosts really exist. Swami is quite clear on that; He says they do: (**Love is My Form**, page 450)

> About the desire to die in troubled times, Baba said that one should live and fight the trouble and not think of death. "You don't know what a nasty state awaits those who commit suicide. Life in the womb is also a bad period. To die before natural death, one should find another body. **This is like finding another house, before vacating the present one.** If you leave your present house without first finding another, you will land on the roads. This is not a joke. Those who leave their bodies by their own will, end up as *prētha* [ghosts]. Real happiness comes fifteen minutes before death and birth"

There's an amusing story of Totapuri "Nangta" Maharaj, the Advaita Vedanta guru of the Master, running into a *bhairava*, an attendant of Lord Shiva, while going into a grove to meditate. The *bhairava* tells him threateningly: "I have been staying at this place for the last seven hundred years." Unfazed, Nangta responds: "Good, then we can meditate together." The *bhairava* laughs and disappears

My kid Niki was narrating a Ouija board experiment at her friend's place one night when things started going wrong spookily

Ballu of Infosys Banking Business Unit once told me a scary one. It happened on the New BEL Road much before the Outer Ring Road was built. It goes as follows:

> This guy was walking back home past the Sadashiv Nagar Police Station when a lady joined him. He thought that it was good to have some company on the desolate stretch. They went together for a while, talking about some general stuff. After some time, the lady said that her house had come and walked **straight through** the hedge into an old house

Man, get the heebie-jeebies just to think of that! The poor guy, he was out for six months and was a bag of bones on a hospital bed by the end of that period

Here's a ghost story with a nice ending. When we were learning French at *L'Alliance Française*, Chennai in 1990, the teacher asked us to tell a short story in French

Mine was: **Le fantôme à Santhome**

Un homme, il visite une vieille grande maison à Santhome. Dans la nuit, il trouve qu'il faut aller de la salle de bains, mais il ne connaît pas son emplacement. Donc il se déplace ça et là dans la grande maison, quand un fantôme se manifeste devant l'homme surpris. Il dit: «Tu sais que j'ai été ici plus de cent ans!» L'homme, il est très cool, il répond: «Peut-être pouvez- vous me donner les directions de la salle de bains»!

A man, he visits an old big house in Santhome. In the night, he finds that he has to go to the bathroom, but he doesn't know its location. So he moves here and there in the big house, when a ghost appears in front of the surprised man. He said, "You know I've been here over a hundred years!" The man, he's very cool, he replies, "Maybe you can give me directions to the bathroom"!

The Elegant Clarifier

Apart from His munificence, Swami has made a couple of phenomenal clarifications that have helped me tremendously

nēti, nēti

nēti loosely translates to "Not this", to imply that the *jnāni* reaches the Self by negation

Swami says that *nēti* actually means "Not only this". I like this translation more and is more in sync with what the Master says in the **Gospel**: (Chapter **21. A Day at Dakshineswar**)

> MASTER: "Jnana is the realization of Self through the process of '*nēti, nēti*', 'Not this, not this'. One goes into *samādhi* through this process of elimination and realizes the *Ātman*

> "But *vijnāna* means Knowledge with a greater fullness. Some have heard of milk, some have seen milk, and some have drunk milk. He who has merely heard of it is 'ignorant'. He who has seen it is a *jnāni*. But he who has drunk it has *vijnāna*, that is to say, a fuller knowledge of it. After having the vision of God one talks to Him as if He were an intimate relative. That is *vijnāna*

"First of all you must discriminate, following the method of '*nēti, nēti*': 'He is not the five elements, nor the sense-organs, nor the mind, nor the intelligence, nor the ego. He is beyond all these cosmic principles.' You want to climb to the roof; then you must eliminate and leave behind all the steps, one by one. The steps are by no means the roof. But after reaching the roof you find that the steps are made of the same materials — brick, lime, and brick-dust — as the roof. It is the Supreme Brahman that has become the universe and its living beings and the twenty-four cosmic principles. That which is *Ātman* has become the five elements. You may ask why the earth is so hard, if it has come out of *Ātman*? All is possible through the will of God. Don't you see that bone and flesh are made from blood and semen? How hard 'sea-foam' becomes!

"After attaining *vijnāna* one can live in the world as well. Then one clearly realizes that God Himself has become the universe and all living beings, that He is not outside the world"

I am intrigued by the acronym (NOT) from Swami's interpretation, which can be expanded endlessly like the Universe! It also reminds me of how GOD is an acronym for "God Over Djinn" in **Gödel, Escher, Bach: an Eternal Golden Braid** by Douglas R Hofstadter [https://g.co/kgs/AE8Vda]

Refuse the Fruit

Though the common interpretation of the generally-quoted verse in the Bhagavad Gita [especially in Obituaries] says that one has no right to the fruit of action, Swami makes one more wonderful distinction:

When one has the right to engage in action, one also has the right over the fruits of that action; no one can deny or refuse this. But the doer can, out of one's own free will and determination, refuse to be affected by the result, whether favorable or unfavorable. The Lord has said in the Geeta, 'refuse the fruit' (*mā phalēshu*), which means, the deed does yield results, but the doer should not do it with the results in view. If Krishna's intention was to say that the doer has no right over the fruits of action, He would have said, 'It is fruitless' or '*nā phalēshu*', (*na*, meaning no). To engage oneself in karma, knowing well that the result will follow, and yet being unattached to it or being unconcerned with it, is the sign of purity~Geeta Vahini, Chapter 5

Omnipresent

This one hit me as soon as i opened the Sanatana Sarathi magazine for the month of August, 2016, above the **Contents**:

> You have mountainous hopes for the future. But the future is not certain. Then why do you bother about those things? Live in the present. It is not an ordinary present; it is omnipresent. Past results are in the present. Future results are also in the present

The full impact of that ॐ**ni** prefix is yet to hit me, but i was in a different realm when i did the pūja later that morning

samasta lōka sukhinō bhavantu

A Mysterious Run of Full Moons

With no full moon in February in 2018, we ended up with two in March, just like in January, and, that too on the same dates: 2nd and 31st!

Quite rare to see two full moons in a month and the reason for the phrase: "Once in a blue moon", normally once in 32 months. 31st March 2018 was the last Blue Moon we'd see for over two years, till Halloween 2020

The full moon at the end of March 2018 started an interesting sequence: with each passing month, the day of the full moon **dropped** by a day

31	March	(Sat)	Chaitra Purnima
30	April	(Mon)	Vaishakha Purnima
29	May	(Tue)	Jyeshtha Purnima
28	June	(Thu)	Jyeshtha Purnima
27	July	(Fri)	Ashadha Purnima
26	August	(Sun)	Shravana Purnima
25	September	(Tue)	Bhadrapada Purnima
24	October	(Wed)	Ashwin Purnima
23	November	(Fri)	Kartik Purnima
22	December	(Sat)	Margashirsha Purnima

Which means that the day and the month added up to a constant: 34, in this case

What's the date of the full moon in November 2018?

Easy, it's the 23rd (34–11), which is the birthday of Swami!

We were in Ankleshwar that evening, on the South bank of the Great River Ma Narmada on our Ma Narmada PariCarMa 2018

For math aficionados, a couple of bonuses:

- 34 is a Fibonacci number
- The last full moon for the year fell on the 131st birth anniversary of **The Man Who Knew Infinity** [Srinivasa Ramanujan]

Folks might object saying that the Lunar Month is about 29½ days, so this sort of thing is bound to happen

My counter to that is that there are intervening months [May, July, August, October] with 31 days and that's why the drop of a day with each month is so elegant; it could very easily go out of whack and that's why i like to refer to it as, Howard Murphet wrote, "fiddling in the *ākāsha*"!

Fan Baba

Early October 2019, it was raining seriously after 2 AM and any chances of playing tennis in the al fresco courts at our gated community got washed away

So slept past the alarms at 5 AM and 6 AM

Got a very interesting dream post that

Some person was in a narrow alley; was chatting with him, when he took out a photo of Swami from his wooden trunk box

Soon, Swami was there in person!

He was reclining and behind Him was a person, who i can't ID now, along with Shirdi Baba

Swami started fanning Himself with a hand fan and i said that i'd do it :-)

Took it from Him and started fanning Him and Shirdi Baba; what joy!

When i woke up, the time was 6:41; Wednesdays are always special

Of late, have been fanning the deities in our Puja Room using a hand fan in the Infinity [∞] loop of the beating wings of the hummingbird, like Captain Mike in The Curious Case of Benjamin Button

The only catch with it: don't know when to stop ;-)

Resairrection

Written the day Swami attained MahāSamādhi
[24th April 2011]

The Infinite One
Cannot be Understood
Only Experienced

Earlier this month, i was wondering: "Hey, did i pray for
His recovery?" I didn't. I wasn't even doing the basic stuff,
even though He's done so much for me as noted in the
**Letter to The Week on their "80th birthday of
Swami" issue**

https://www.saibabaofindia.com/feb2008/sai_baba_shivaratri_calendar1440.jpg

March 2008

Sun	Mon	Tue	Wed	Thu	Fri	Sat
						1
2	3	4	5	6	7	8
9	10	11	12	13	14	15
16	17	18	19	20	21	22
23	24	25	26	27	28	29
30	31					

May the blessings of Lord Sai Shiva...
Always be with you!

SAIBABAOFINDIA.COM

Some of His great observations:

- Puttaparthi stands for "Put-apart-the-i"
- Properties are not proper ties
- Television is actually tele-*visham* (poison). Research has shown that frequent viewing dulls the left (logical) brain
- Even though *nēti, nēti* has generally been translated as "Not this, Not this", Swami has given the better interpretation: "Not only this, Not only this", which can be abbreviated to NOT and expanded endlessly liked the Universe (like God = God over djinn, in Gödel, Escher, Bach by Douglas Hofstadter)
- When Prof. Venkatraman, who wrote Sai Baba's **Final Days - An Eyewitness Account** and many other interesting articles, met Swami for the first time, Swami asked him: "What do you want?" The professor said: "I want peace", to which Swami responded: "Drop the I and the want, and you'll have Peace"!

Some of His humor:

- To a devotee who wanted Swami to give him a haircut: "I am Baba, not barber"
- To a devotee with a BA: "You're a BA, I am a double BA"
- When someone wanted Swami to materialize something alive, He created a monkey that pranced & "pranked" about and disappeared after a while

On **Wednesday** 22nd September 2004, He saved me from a monetary jam within the space of 12 hours when i cried in front of His photo in our *pūja* room and, at the end of that month, showed us His Third Eye

This is the reason why 09/22 is such a dear date to me

The fact that it gels so well with the eponymous verse in the Bhagavad-Gita is the icing!

On *Sri Rāma Navami* in 2007 [March 27th], my father-in-law and i found a masterpiece set of 163 Sundaram Sai bhajans, which i still listen to

Here's one of my favorites: *Sai Baba Gita Sudha* (in Telugu script)

Probably, in my heart of hearts, i feel that He's the Formless. Don't know for sure, but this really made me understand what He once said:

The ananth is an anāth
(The Infinite is an orphan)

"Yes, for you, you have Sai. You will pray to Him and get any work done by Him. But whom shall I call? I have no Sai. I am *anāth*"

The Master explains the mystery of the Incarnation in his inimitable way in the **Gospel**: (Chapter **26. Festival at Adhar's House**)

Even a judge, while giving evidence in a case, comes down and stands in the witness-box

Given that we are right on Easter, what could be more fitting than Swami resurrecting like Jesus and living on for 96 years as has been predicted...

Be that as it may, Swami is always close to Me and cheering me up through this photo in the room of the kids

Sunlight on Swami
The eyes have It

From **Chapter 30** of the **Shri Sai Satcharita**:

On reaching the place, Kakaji went to the Masjid, and fell at Baba's Feet. His eyes were soon bedewed with tears, and his mind attained calmness. According to the vision of the Goddess, no sooner did he see Baba, that his mind lost all its restlessness and it became calm and composed. Kakaji began to think, in his mind, "What a wonderful power is this! Baba spoke nothing, there was no question and answer, no benediction pronounced; the mere *darshan* itself was so conducive to happiness; the restlessness of my mind disappeared by His mere *darshan*, consciousness of joy came upon me - this is what is called 'the greatness of darshan'"

The words of Ramanachala are still ringing in my ears:

To devotees who begged him to cure himself for the sake of his followers, Sri Ramana is said to have replied, "Why are you so attached to this body? Let it go", and, "Where can I go? I am here"

About the Author

Srinivas Shastri was born in Vizag in 1965, on the edge of Infinity, with Ramakrishna Beach separating his house on a promontory from the Bay of Bengal, the largest bay in the world

He studied Mechanical Engineering at Andhra University College of Engineering and majored in Systems and Finance at IIM, Ahmedabad in the mid~1980s

Work was a bit of a shock for him. Somehow he did about 19 years of that, before retiring in 2006 for good. The best experience was working on the Executive Search app for Maars India, where he gleaned many nuggets about the Net, such as **asynchronous** design

This is his sixth blook, after:

1. *Brushes with Brahmn ~ Dancing with my Datta* [https://g.co/kgs/9qycik]
2. *Ma Narmada PariCarMa ~ A Pictorial Essay of a Parikrama* [https://g.co/kgs/VXDaLx]
3. *Ramanachala ~ Impact of Sri Ramana Maharshi* [https://g.co/kgs/G1tjdz]
4. *Ramakrishna ~ A Maverick of a Mystic* [https://www.amazon.in/dp/B09T6Q5NF1/]
5. *Shirdi Sai Baba ~ An Akshayapātra* [https://www.amazon.com/dp/B0B4HN3L6X]